My First
1000
WORDS

Illustrated by
JUDY HENSMAN

Brown Watson
ENGLAND

contents

ISBN 0-7097-1086-0
First Published 1996
Reprinted 1997
Published by Brown Watson
The Old Mill, 76 Fleckney Road
Kibworth Beauchamp
Leicestershire, England

father, dad, husband

mother, mum, wife

grandfather (father's father)

ndmother (her's mother)

son, brother

daughter, sister

cousin (aunt's daughter)

cousin (uncle's son)

nt (mother's sister)

uncle (mother's brother)

our bodies

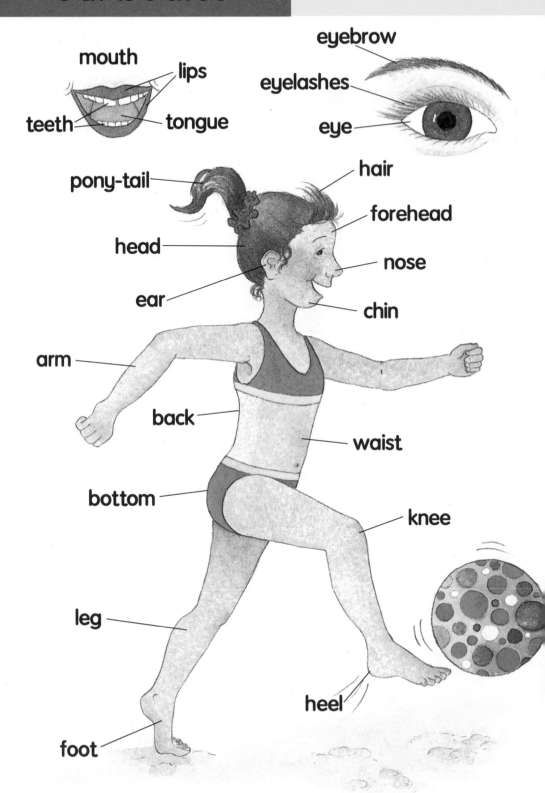

mouth

lips

teeth

tongue

eyebrow

eyelashes

eye

pony-tail

hair

forehead

head

nose

ear

chin

arm

back

waist

bottom

knee

leg

heel

foot

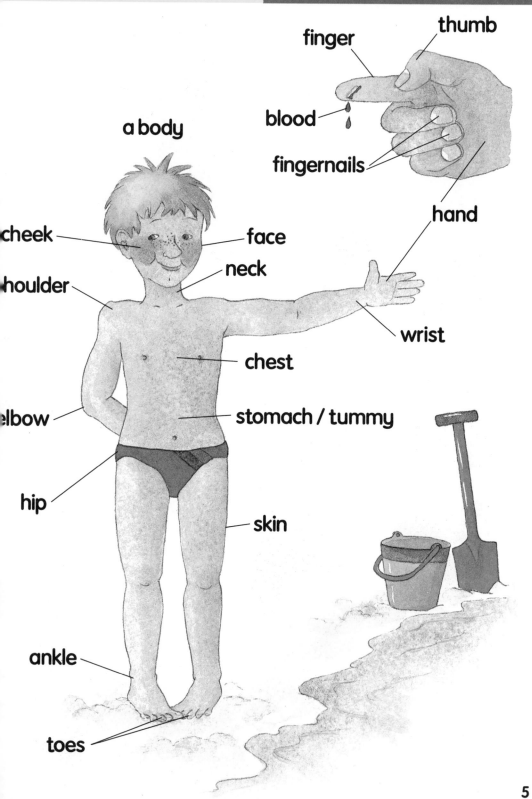

thumb

finger

blood

fingernails

hand

a body

cheek

face

shoulder

neck

wrist

chest

elbow

stomach / tummy

hip

skin

ankle

toes

more people words

bald

people

moustache

parents

beard

man

boy

bride

hear

taste

twins

bridegroom

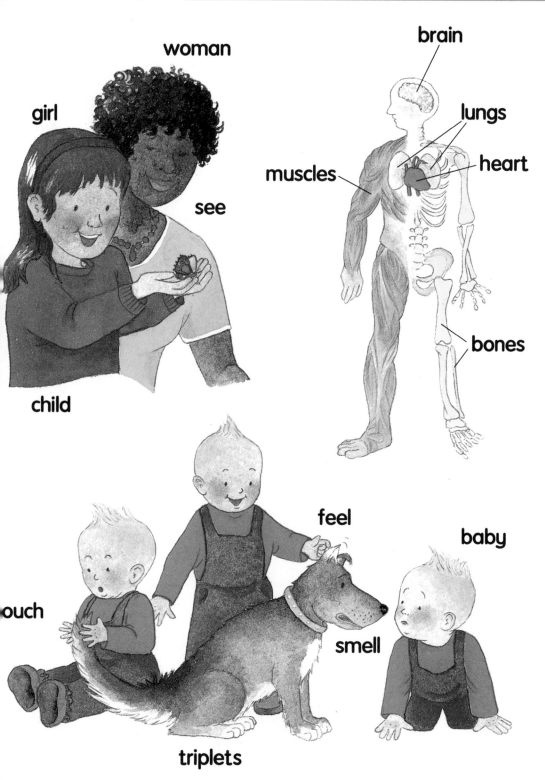

woman

girl

see

child

brain

lungs

muscles

heart

bones

feel

baby

ouch

smell

triplets

clothes

 dress

jumper

 hat

knickers 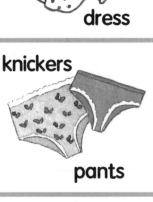 pants

 dressing gown

 trousers

 anorak

socks

blouse

 skirt

pyjamas

petticoat

leggings

coat

cap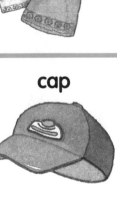

shorts

raincoat

T-shirt

tights

vest

jacket

nightdress

jeans

scarf

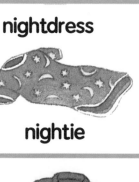
nightie

nderpants

cardigan

rainhat

sweater

shirt

track suit

more things to wear

laces

slippers

earrings

buttonhole

tie

handkerchief/ hankie

braces

button

suit

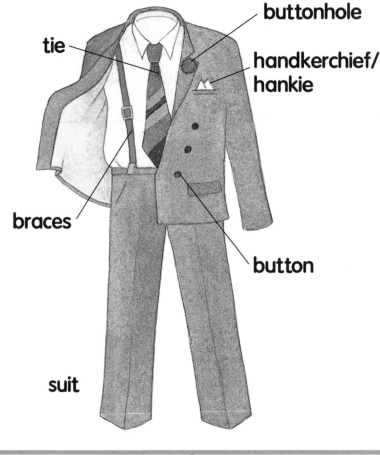

necklace

rubber boots

glasses

shoes

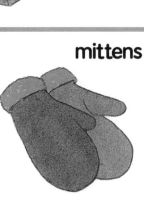

mittens

apr

more things to wear

overalls

gloves

ring

trainers

belt

boots

buckle

tiara

swimsuit

ribbon

hairband

sandals

brooch

bracelet

trunks

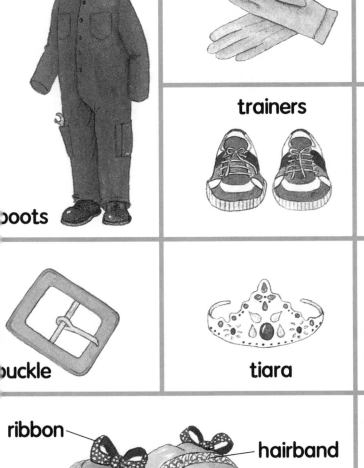
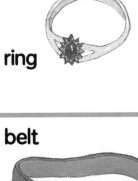
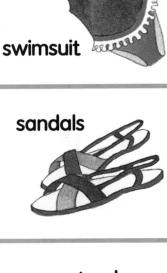

the bedroom

 **bedside table**

 **lamp**

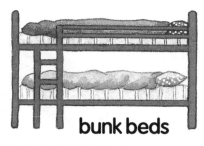 **bunk beds**

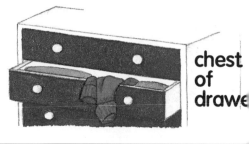 **chest of drawe**

 **eiderdown**

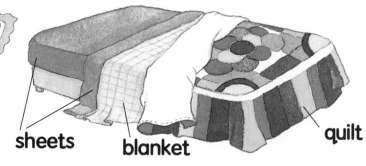 **sheets** **blanket** **quilt**

the bedroom

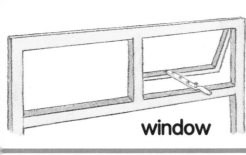
window

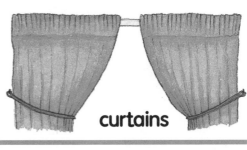
curtains

alarm
clock

wardrobe

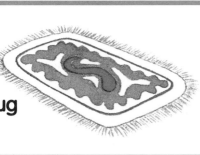
rug

bed

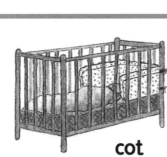
cot

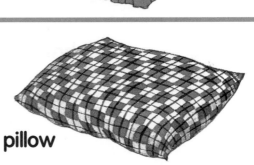
pillow

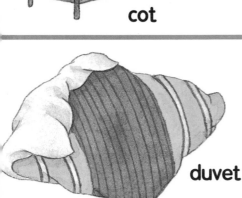
duvet

cradle

13

the bathroom

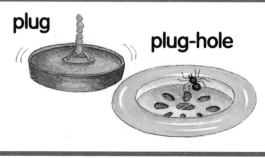

plug

plug-hole

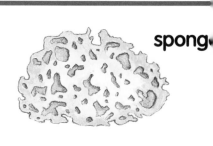

spong

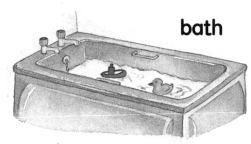

bath

bubbles

toilet

toilet paper

wash-basin

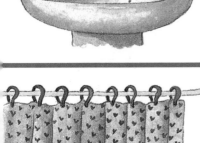

towel

shower-curtain

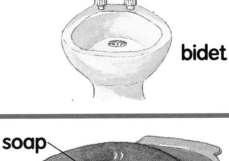

bidet

towel-rail

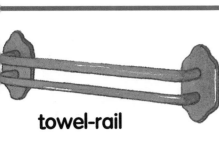

soap

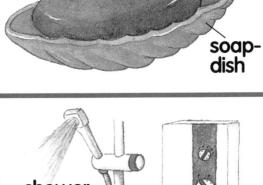

soap-dish

othpaste

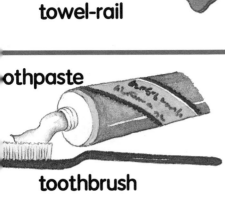

toothbrush

shower

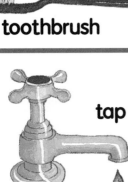

tap

potty

15

food-mixer

kettle

coffee pot

cupboard

cooker

oven

draining board

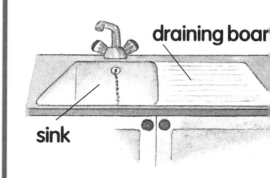

sink

teapot

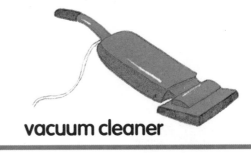

vacuum cleaner

iron

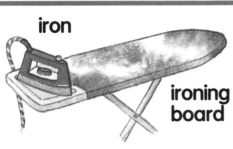

ironing board

washing machine

dish-washer

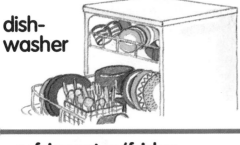

switch

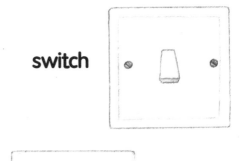

refrigerator/fridge

socket

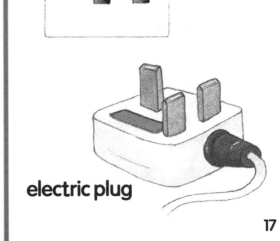

electric plug

freezer

the living-room

books

book-ends

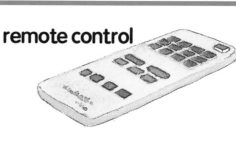

remote control

hi-fi system

vase of flowers

door-handle

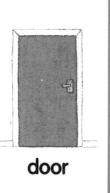

door

gas fire

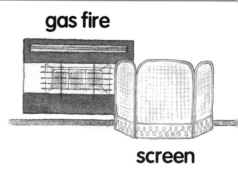

screen

painting

magazine rack

newspapers

comics

magazines

telephone/phone

video cassette

video recorder

television set /TV

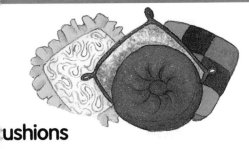

ushions

photographs

mantelpiece

fireplace

radio

19

the dining-room

table-cloth

plates

cup

saucer

teaspoon

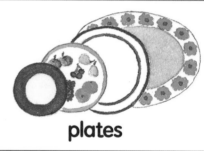

vinegar

oil

mirror

napkin ring

napkins

fork

spoon

table-mat

knife

candles

candlestick

pepper

salt

chairs

dining-table

eggcups

jug

tumbler

fruit bowl

wine-glasses

bottle

21

the playroom

rocking horse

soft toys

playpen

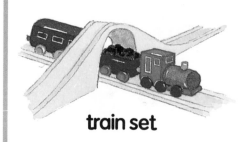
train set

building blocks

toy soldiers

fort

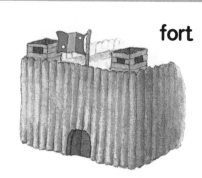

the playroom

toy duck

toy boats

spinning top

teddy bear

toy cars

counting frame

skittles

doll's house

playhouse

doll's pram

things in the house

hatstand

settee/sofa

bench

armchair

beanbag

footstool

rug

stool

rocking-chair

high-chair

things in the house

bookcase

table lamp

ideboard

grandfather clock

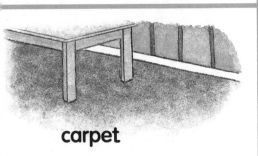

carpet

coffee table

candelabra

dressing-table

breakfast bar

the garden

greenhouse

shed

hedge

watering-can

compost heap

dustbin

vegetable plot

rake

bushes

wheelbarrow

garden fork

spade

flower-bed

sprinkler

hoe

flowers

chimney

TV aerial

roof

bonfire

drain-pipe

gutter

porch

ladder

front door

window box

barrel

roof tiles

grass lawn

path

lawnmower

hosepipe

in the workshop

ramp

tyres

car jack

tyre lever

foot-pump

car battery

paint-brushes

saw

sandpaper

paint pots

nuts and bolts

file

spanners

pickaxe

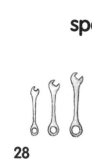

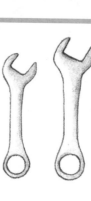

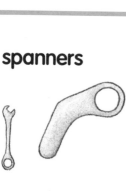

28

can

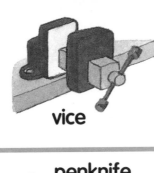
vice

axe

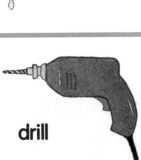
drill

penknife

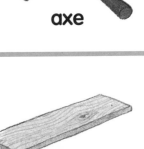
wooden plank

screwdriver

screws
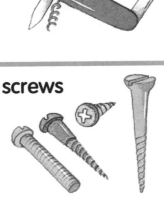

bucket

toolbox

plane
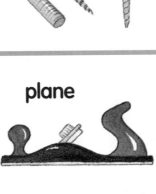

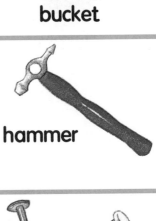
hammer

tape-measure

pliers

nails

friendly pets

mouse

toad

hamster

rat

frog

guinea-pig

gerbil

rabbit

basket

cat

kitten

tortoise

fishbowl

kennel

newt

goldfish

terrapin

dog

puppy

hedgehog

silkworm

stick-insect

budgerigar

canary

lizard

pigeon

lovebirds

mynah bird

horse

birdcage

parrot

foal

Shetland pony

out in the street

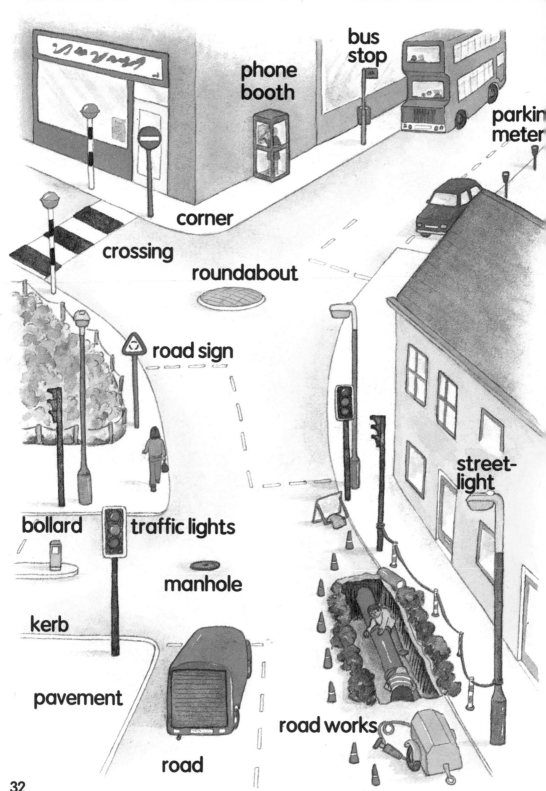

phone booth

bus stop

parking meter

corner

crossing

roundabout

road sign

street-light

bollard

traffic lights

manhole

kerb

pavement

road works

road

bicycle

bus

fire-engine

taxi

car

road-roller

lorry

motor-
cycle

police car

van

in town

church

restaurant

market

houses

hotel

skyscraper

post office

shop

car park

theatre

bank

factory

pub

park

school

supermarket

library

cinema

police station

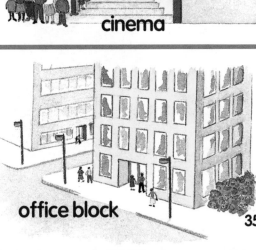

office block

in the supermarket

breakfast cereal

sausages

meat

chicken

ham

fruit juice

eggs

jam

fish

chocolate bars

turnstile

cans of beans

cheese

butter

milk

till

credit card

money

receipt

check-out desk

trolley

purse

handbag

shopping bag

all kinds of fruit

orange

grapes

banana

cherries

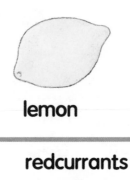
lemon

pineapple

apple

redcurrants

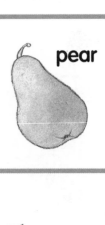
plums

gooseberries
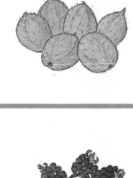

grapefruit

pear

blackberries

melon

strawberries

abbage

tomatoes

cucumber

potatoes

pumpkin

peas

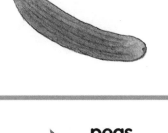

corn on the cob

carrots

onions

leeks

green beans

cauliflower

lettuce

mushrooms

sprouts

39

more things to eat and drink

cake

hot dog

rice

jelly

honey

coconut

packet of
spaghetti

toast

milk
shake

doughnuts

lollipop

jellybabies

fish fingers

pancakes

bottle of cola

more things to eat and drink

ice-cream

buns

sausage roll

nuts

bag of sugar

chips

bar of chocolate

tomato sauce

salad

apple pie

can of soup

biscuits

sandwich

loaf of bread

pizza

fun in the park

kite

railings

litter-bin

notice board

bandstand

picnic

park
keeper

scooter

sand-pit

fountain

pond

toy yacht

swings

climbing frame

slide

see-saw

roundabout

skipping rope

path

helmet

drinking fountain

roller skates

pads

skateboard

lead

collar

dog muzzle

people at work

actor

secretary

musician

gardener

decorator

shop-keeper

astronaut

diver

cook

singer

dancer

hairdresser

artist

baker

postman

farmer

carpenter

butcher

more people at work

fisherman

nurse

teacher

miner

waiter

bricklayer

plumber

explorer

dentist

clown

judge

porter

TV announcer

window cleaner

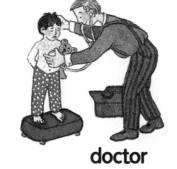
doctor

fireman

scientist

electrician
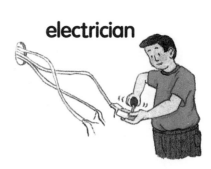

47

in the office

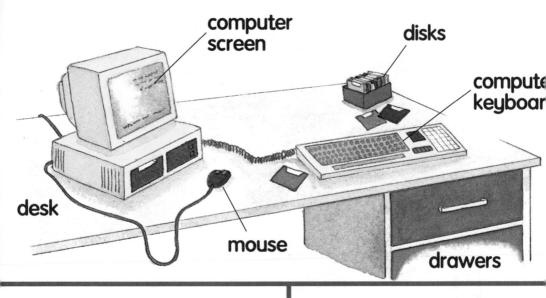

computer screen

disks

computer keyboard

desk

mouse

drawers

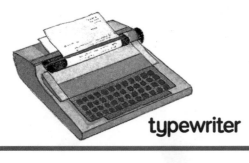

typewriter

electric fan

swivel chair

fax machine

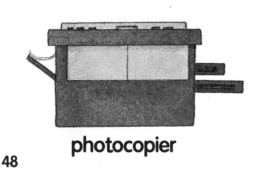

photocopier

writing paper

envelopes

48

calendar

filing cabinet

pencil

pen
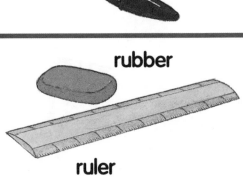

pencil sharpener

rubber

ruler
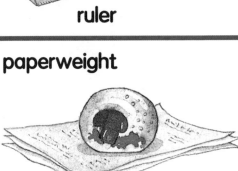

stapler
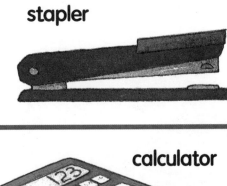

paperweight

calculator
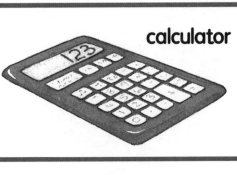

wastepaper bin

coffee machine
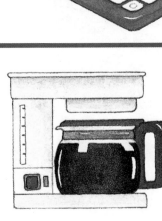

at the garage

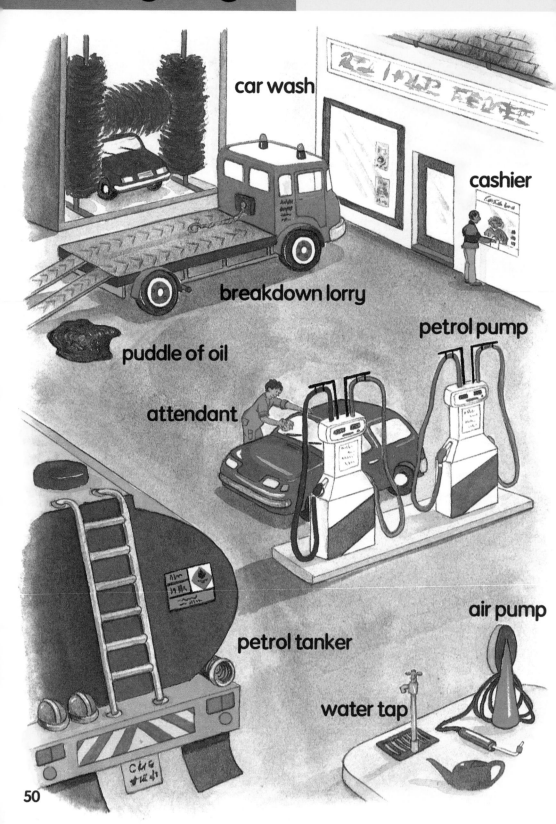

car wash

cashier

breakdown lorry

puddle of oil

petrol pump

attendant

petrol tanker

air pump

water tap

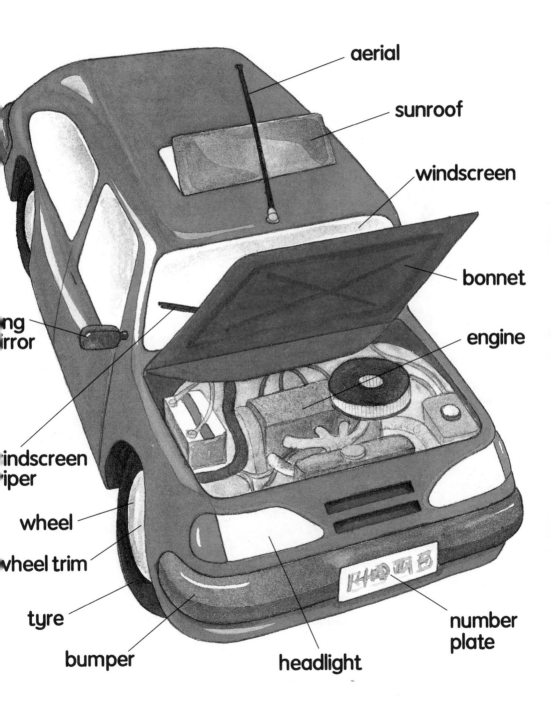

aerial

sunroof

windscreen

bonnet

engine

...ng ...irror

...indscreen ...iper

wheel

...heel trim

tyre

bumper

headlight

number plate

51

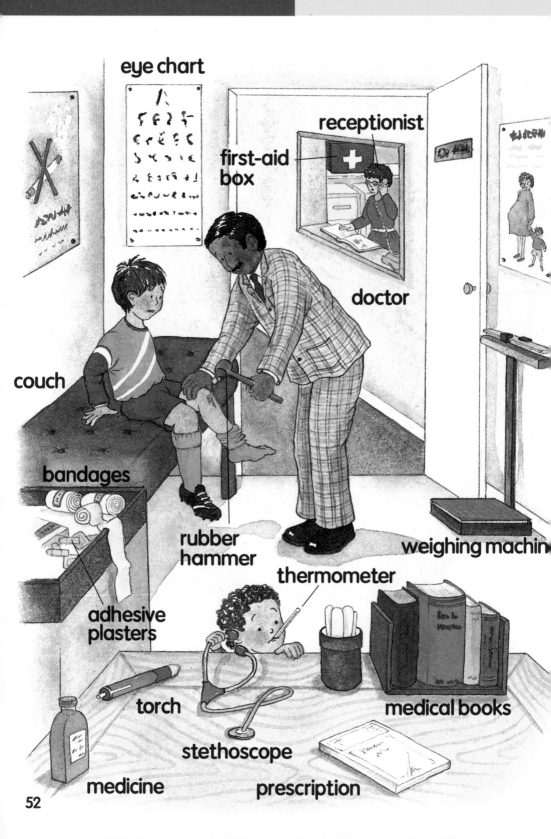

eye chart

receptionist

first-aid box

doctor

couch

bandages

rubber hammer

weighing machin[e]

thermometer

adhesive plasters

torch

medical books

stethoscope

medicine

prescription

52

at the dentist

big smile

bright light

dentist

fillings

dental nurse

record chart

mask

drill

glass of mouthwash

bib

gown

probe

dentist's mirror

dentist's chair

false teeth

in hospital

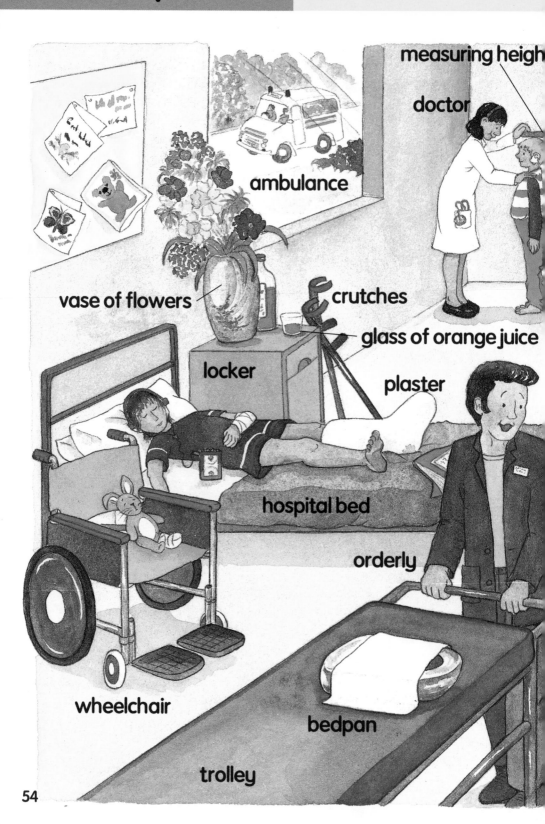

measuring height

doctor

ambulance

vase of flowers

crutches

glass of orange juice

locker

plaster

hospital bed

orderly

wheelchair

bedpan

trolley

lift

X-RAY DEPT.

DO NOT ENTER
WHEN RED
LIGHT IS ON

x-ray
machine

x-ray

curtain

consultant

nurse

chart

syringe

tray

potty

slippers

scissors

55

games and pastimes

reading

writing

blindman's buff

Best Ghost Stories

dressing-up

sewing

singing

board game

collecting stamps

sleeping

chess

computer game

walking

listening to music

dancing

playing cards

leapfrog

making music

gardening

sports

canoeing

American football

diving

tennis

showjumping

basketball

skating

rugby

cycling

58

gymnastics

swimming

baseball

skiing

cricket

running

table tennis

football

horse-riding

on the farm

sheep   lamb

cow

calf

ducklings   duck

milk
churns

orchard

cockerel

on the farm

haystack

turkey

goslings goose

foal horse

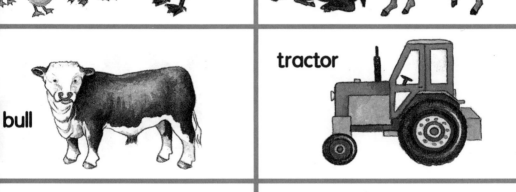
bull

tractor

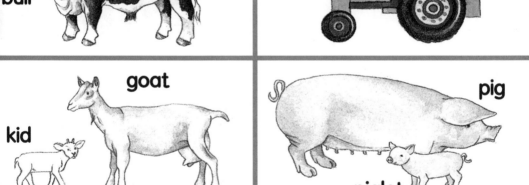
goat
kid

pig
piglet

hen chicks

field
fence

at school

lunch-box

pupils

globe

pot of paste

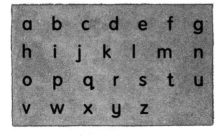

a b c d e f g
h i j k l m n
o p q r s t u
v w x y z

alphabet

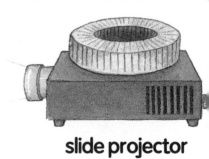

slide projector

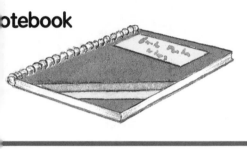

wall chart

notebook

teacher

blackboard

easel

satchel

duster

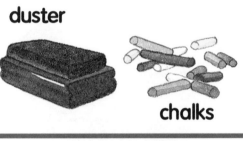

chalks

drawing

pencil case

modelling clay

writing

going places: by train

signal

the railway station

platform

buffer

passenger

ticket collector

escalator

diesel engine

level crossing

railway line

goods wagon

carria

going places: by train

ticket office

buffet car

porter

luggage

tunnel

underground railway

monorail

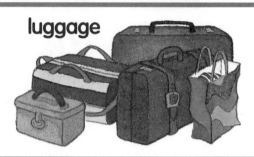

signal box

smoke

steam engine

65

going places: by water

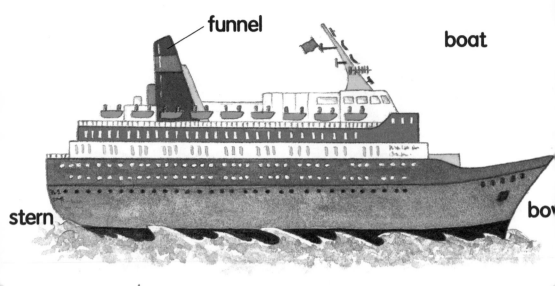

funnel

boat

stern

bow

mast

tug-boat

yacht

submarine

anchor

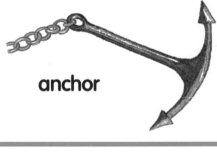

buoy

hydrofoil

going places: by water

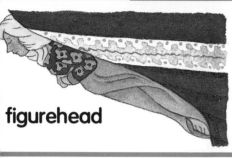

figurehead

rowing boat — **oar**

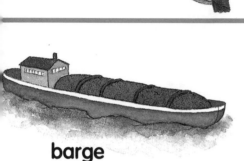

barge

hovercraft

paddle-steamer

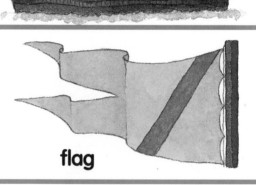

flag

speedboat

ferry-boat

houseboat

sails

67

going places: by plane

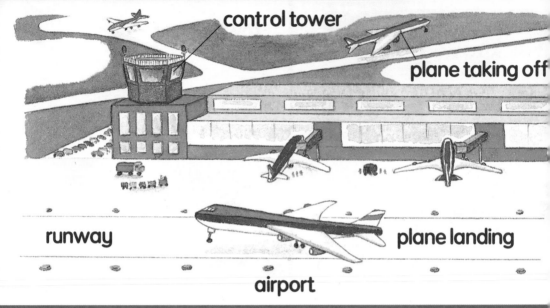

control tower

plane taking off

runway

plane landing

airport

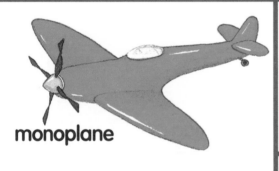

monoplane

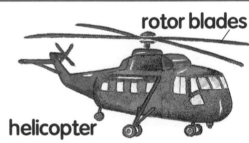

rotor blades

helicopter

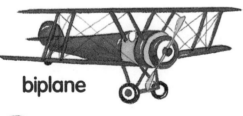

biplane

fuel tanker

triplane

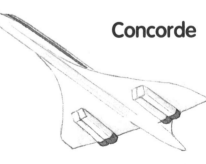

Concorde

going places: by plane

air hostess

seaplane

passenger jet

propeller

light aircraft

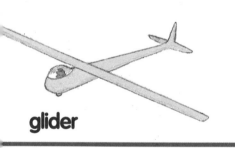
glider

jumbo jet

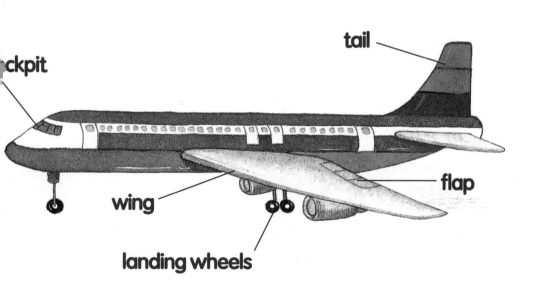
tail

cockpit

wing

flap

landing wheels

in the country

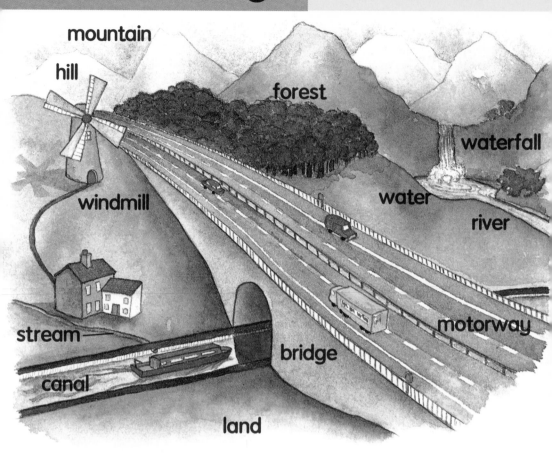

mountain

hill

forest

waterfall

windmill

water

river

stream

motorway

canal

bridge

land

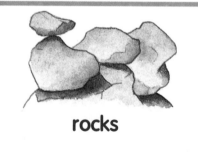

rocks

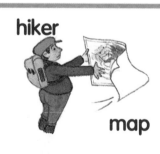

hiker

map

caravan

tent

camper

campfire

sleeping bag

70

fishing rod

ing net

fisherman

trees

arecrow

wild flowers

stepping stones

village

town

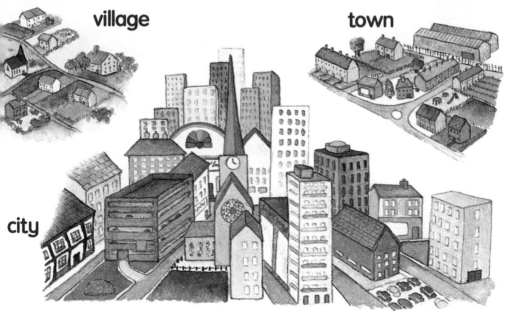

city

builders and buildings

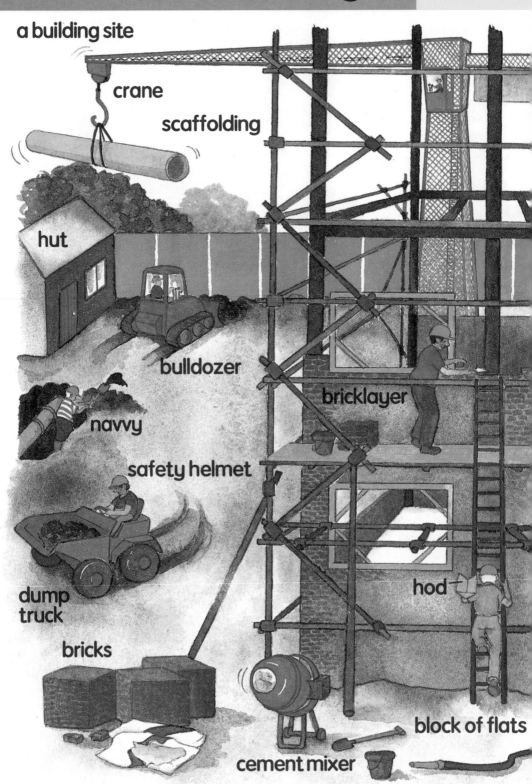

a building site

crane

scaffolding

hut

bulldozer

navvy

safety helmet

dump truck

bricks

bricklayer

hod

block of flats

cement mixer

builders and buildings

fire station

terraced houses

cottage

mosque

car park

hospital

art gallery

hangar

stately home

boathouse

museum

tower

73

seasons and weather

winter

spring

lightning

sunshine

summer

autumn

rainbow

rai

storm

hail

ice

snow

74

tiny animals

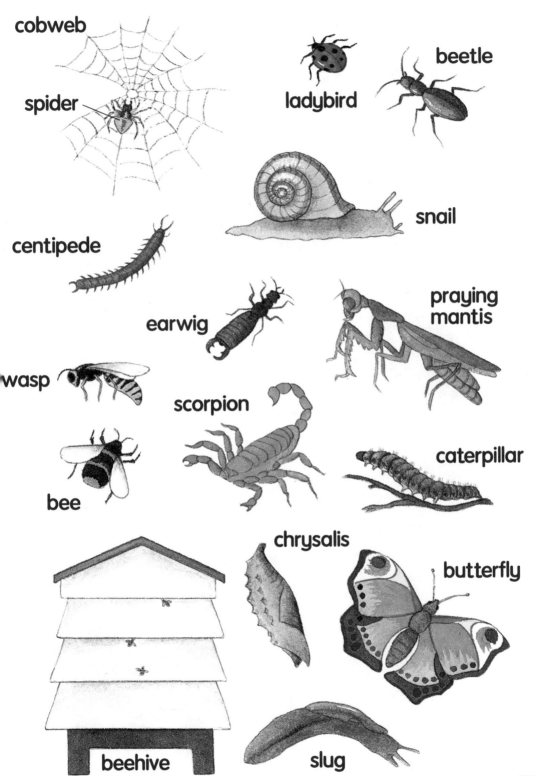

cobweb

spider

ladybird

beetle

snail

centipede

earwig

praying mantis

wasp

scorpion

bee

caterpillar

chrysalis

butterfly

beehive

slug

wild animals

peacock

owl

monkey

ostrich

tiger

giraffe

lion

elephant

gorilla

penguin

woodpecker

stork

swan

porcupine

panda

crocodile

zebra

rhinoceros/rhino

hippopotamus/hippo

whale

octopus

dolphin

lobster

swordfish

manta ray

moose

shark

camel

polar bear

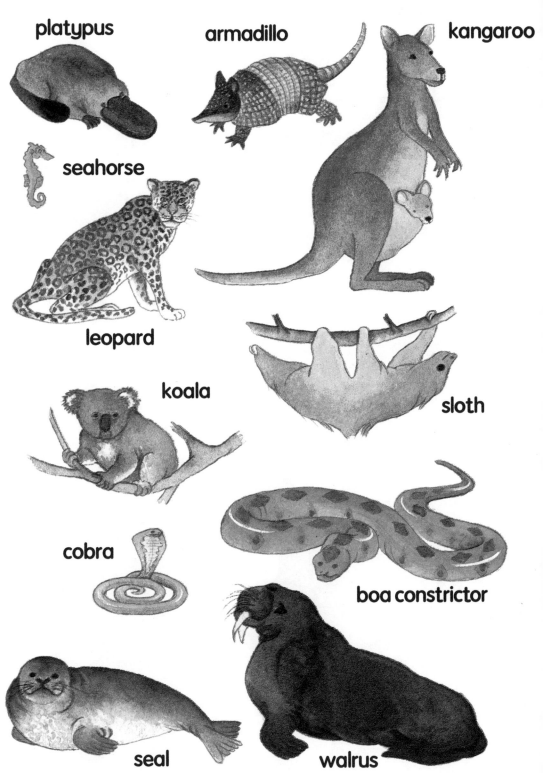

platypus

armadillo

kangaroo

seahorse

leopard

koala

sloth

cobra

boa constrictor

seal

walrus

animal parts

wing

feather

antlers

beak

tail

whiskers

hoof

fin

paw

sh

flipper

pouch

hump

tusl

trunk

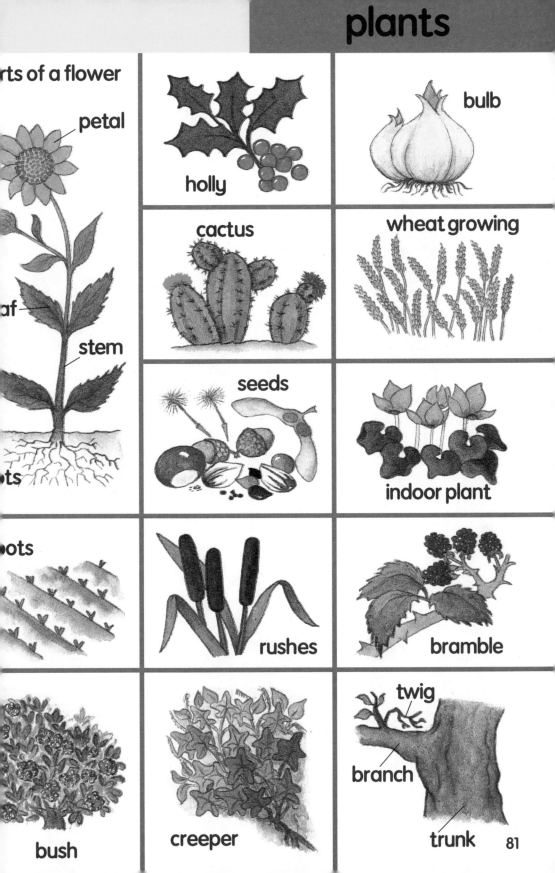

rts of a flower

petal

leaf

stem

ots

holly

cactus

seeds

bulb

wheat growing

indoor plant

ots

rushes

bramble

bush

creeper

twig

branch

trunk

81

beside the sea

seagulls

boatman

water-skier

donkey

windsurfer

crab

mussels

shellfish

jellyfish

seaweed

pool

starfish

sandcastle

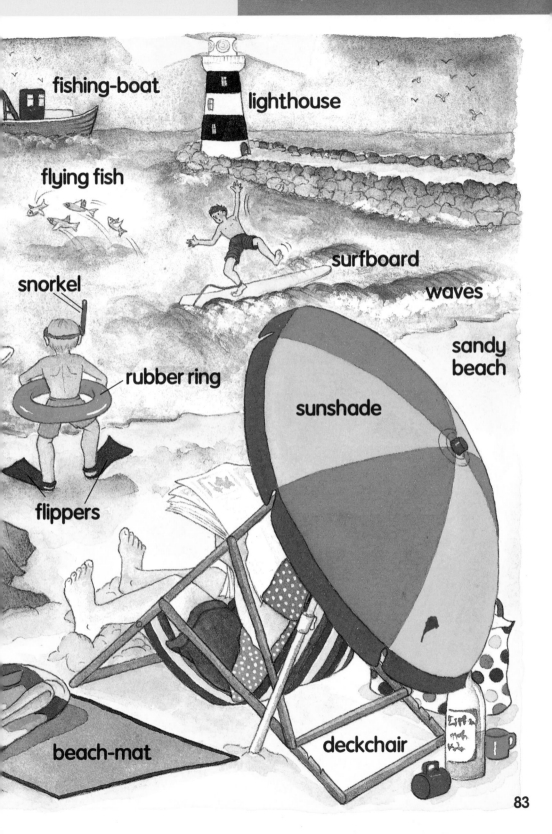

fishing-boat

lighthouse

flying fish

surfboard

waves

snorkel

sandy beach

rubber ring

sunshade

flippers

beach-mat

deckchair

having a party

paper chain

balloons

cloa

paper hat

birthday cards

candles

iced cake

sweets

biscuits

sandwiches

crackers

fizzy drinks

chocolates

straws

crumbs

sparklers

magician

party
invitation

Please come
to my fancy
dress party

hostess

guest

presents

ribbon

fancy dress costumes

opposites

over

under

in

out

happy

sad

up

down

high

low

wet

dry

opposites

fast

slow

fat

thin

big

small

above

below

behind

in front

pirate

witch

dwarf

ghost

fairy

dragon

giant

wizard

mermaid

dinosaur

88

colours and shapes

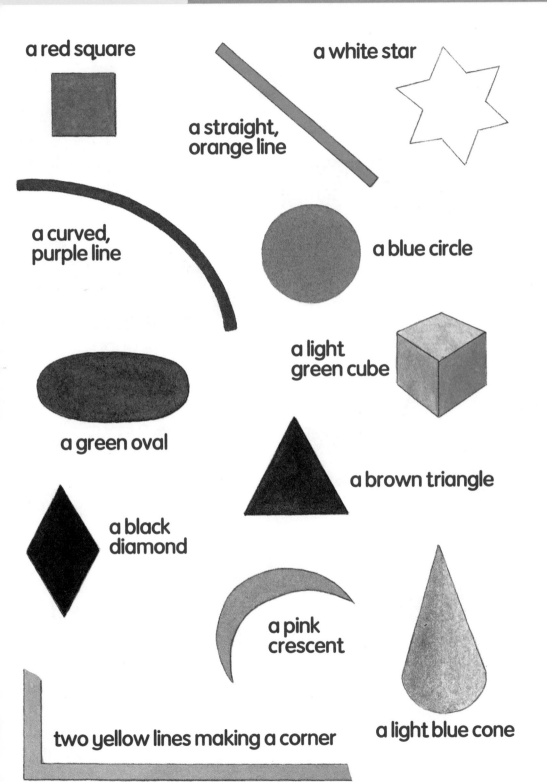

a red square

a white star

a straight, orange line

a curved, purple line

a blue circle

a light green cube

a green oval

a brown triangle

a black diamond

a pink crescent

two yellow lines making a corner

a light blue cone

numbers

1 one girl

2 two boys

3 three ponies

4 four cows

5 five puppies

6 six kittens

7 seven lambs

8 eight pigs

9 nine ducks

10 ten mice